SPIRITUAL CANON

Guidlines to Spirituality

By: His Grace Bishop Seraphim

Bishop of Ismaelia

St Shenouda Coptic Orthodox Monastery

Putty, NSW, Australia

ISBN: 978-0-9805171-7-0

Title: Spiritual Canon: Guidlines to Spirituality

Author: His Grace Bishop Seraphim

Bishop of Ismaelia

Published by: St Shenouda Coptic Orthodox Monastery

8419 Putty Rd Putty, N.S.W. 2330

Sydney, Australia

www.stshenoudamonastery.org

TABLE OF CONTENTS

INTRODUCTION

Spiritual Canon is an extensive and broad subject. It is not limited to the Canonical prayers or Jesus' prayer or even genuflecting, (Matania), neither is it the reading of the Bible and spiritual books, nor adhering to the Sacraments of Confession and Eucharist. It is more intense than that.

Spiritual Canon should be an agreement between a person and his father in confession. It is a meticulous application and adherence to what is agreed upon between them.

Spiritual life cannot be segregated. It is the culmination of all of the above! Thus it is difficult to discuss the topic thoroughly in one booklet. We should not be concerned only with the external appearance of the Spiritual Canon: counting how many times we prayed or how well we recited. More importantly is the spirit by which we carry out our spiritual practices.

On the whole, it is a spiritual training trying to develop and strengthen the method of worship. Its fundamental aim is to rejoice and experience the love of our Lord Jesus Christ, by being continually in His presence.

As the entire Canon is spiritual and not worldly, so it contains many topics which should be touched upon. The aim of this booklet is not to suggest the numbers of spiritual practices, but rather to clarify some important methods of practising the Spiritual rules. As for the details, this should be left to the father in confession, according to the spiritual level of the individual.

Spiritual Rule represents our spiritual image which is the reflection of Jesus Christ. We place this in God's hand to draw us closer to Him. It will unite our will to His holy will; and entitles us, by His grace, to be His children.

May our Lord enlighten us and bestow on us His grace to practice these Rules. May the Holy Spirit pave the path and help us in our spiritual walk all the days of our lives. Amen.

Bishop Seraphim

1 - The Meaning of the Word Canon and its Importance

The word canon means law. It has various meanings in different languages but they all have a common meaning: 'A law by which we lead our spiritual lives.'

Spiritual Canon has different levels. It is essential that the father in confession leads his child cautiously and gradually, according to the spiritual level of each person.

The word Canon also means rule and order. Thus it is important that our exercises have to be acceptable and under a certain rule. The word rule is derived from the word ruler. A ruler helps regulate and measure things. Thus, the spiritual rule should be used to measure our spiritual struggle and progress. Another meaning for ruler is a person who carries and executes rules and laws. Therefore, Spiritual Canon should regulate, rule and guide us in our spiritual journey.

Therefore, the Spiritual Canon is a method of facilitating our spiritual walk to reach the desired goal. The main aim, behind these rules, is to enjoy and delight in God's love.

Through these we understand the importance of the Spiritual Canon. Take for example the body. The body has many limbs. Each limb has its specific function. If the limb does not perform its function, it causes sever illness. For example, an organ which excretes hormones, if it emits more or less hormone as required, the body will suffer different illnesses.

Consequently, God also created man, in His image and likeness, with spiritual resources, in order to employ these spiritual assets for worship and to enjoy a close relationship with the Lord.

Consider the firmament and nature how they are controlled by the Creator! They all follow specific natural patterns. If any goes contrary to its designated function, natural disaster will occur, like the unpredictable floods etc...

Furthermore, rules set by men of authority: example traffic lights, taxation, court justice etc all these are organised to regulate justice and maintain order among people.

From all the above examples we learn that everything has to be organised by certain rules, to facilitate order and stability! Otherwise contrary results will occur.

If that is the case for worldly matters, how much more should we regulate our spiritual rules to maintain our spiritual and social behaviour?

II - WHAT IS THE SPIRITUAL CANON?

Spiritual Canon is a rule which regulates our spiritual life; our spiritual behaviour and our spiritual responsibilities. It maintains our entire spiritual drive.

In the monastery, for example, there are rules regulating the monastic life; be it in communal gathering or in the privacy of the cell. These regulations have to be adhered to, even in the solitude of the wilderness.

Rules were set from a long time ago. There were rules lived by Saints like abba Pachomius, Abba Shenouda, Abba Anthony, Abba Macarius, St Basil and many others. All their spiritual rules were extracted from the Holy Bible. Thus, the rules of those saints were based on the Scripture by following and adhering closely to the commandments.

These rules were instituted by the saints, as a result of the fruit of their long experiences and struggle. They received them by the commandments, by the guidance of the Holy Spirit. It is not strange that other saints, from different nations, lived by the same rules, as they were handed down from one person to the other.

God has facilitated all means to bring us closer to Him. Thus, through the rules we abide by the Lord's commandments, which in turn lead us to a spiritual life acceptable to the Lord.

Furthermore, besides reading the Bible, praying from the Aghbia, reading holy books and fasting, there are other important factors to enhance all these - controlling the thoughts and senses. If there are rules to control our relationship with people; how could there not be rules to control our relationship with God? And if there are rules to control our behaviour and actions, how could there not be rules to control our spiritual behaviour, on which depend our eternity?

III - THE AIM OF SPIRITUAL CANONS

The main aim of monastic rule, consecration rule or any Christian rule is to assist the person to be spiritually conscious, enjoying the love of God and man. Therefore, it generates the desire to reach eternal life.

Thus, the Spiritual Canon helps discern the right path from the wrong; and aids to differentiate between good and evil. Thus, it leads us to the correct course of life. It is like a scale, without which we could go astray. Therefore, we should rejoice that we have such rules to wake us up, whenever we drift or become languid. These rules become law for self-assessment, by which we measure our walk with God and man. Without them we can never assess our spiritual level!

Therefore, The Spiritual Canon satisfies our inner spiritual hunger and thirst, as it is the spiritual food for our souls. It endeavours to uphold our spiritual life. If we desire to be perfect in any kind of sport, guitar or piano - it is essential, at the beginning, to practice daily in order to reach the desired level. Same with our Canon we need to devoutly practice it in order to improve our spiritual lives and be ready to face the intrigues of Satan. It is similar to daily military exercises, holding out weapons of prayer ready for war at any time.

Thus, Spiritual Canon is the ladder which leads us to heaven. It gives us a taste of eternal life, where we will abide eternally in God's presence.

IV - FLEXIBILITY OF THE SPIRITUAL CANON

Worldly rules are rigid and have no room for change. As for the Spiritual rules, although they are compulsory and we are committed to abide by them, at the same time they are flexible. They are set for the sake of man and not man for the sake of rules. It is a means and not an end in itself.

In spite of its flexibility we have to be alert and need to be directed and advised at all times; or else we could fall in the pit of apathy or pride. We abide by the spirit of the rule and not by the rule itself. This spirit has to have a sort of flexibility and be accompanied by spiritual joy.

God judges the person according to his circumstanced, ability and talent. In the parable of the 'talents' (Math 25:15)

He gave each according to his ability. Likewise, the Spiritual Canon has to be according to the person's spiritual level and capability.

Spiritual Canon is like medicine which the doctor prescribes, according to the condition of the sick person. This medicine can vary from one person to the other. This flexibility, in the spiritual rule, helps continuity and stability in all circumstances.

Rules or segment can change but the target never does! The aim is our salvation by which we reach the love of the Lord.

V - Spiritual Canon and Free Will

Is the Spiritual Canon a means of slavery? Is it compulsory? Is it an obligation or a requirement? Not at all! It is an important and beneficial exercise for our salvation. Keeping and abiding by the rules mean submitting our free will and condescending to God's will. Because His will is always the best for our salvation. As the Bible says, "the kingdom of heaven suffers violence, and the violent take it by force." (Matt 11:12)

The spiritual father should not enforce the rule on his children in confession, but rather advices, directs, encourages and convinces them. Thus, the rule should be exercised convincingly with free will and joy. At the same time we have to force ourselves in keeping it, so that we can get used in exercising it with ease.

God gave a rule (command) to Adam and Eve and pointed out the danger of lack of commitment to the command and left it up to their free will. He did the same with Cain.

There is no enforced rule in Christianity. We are created with a free will, but unfortunately, sometimes our free will is not according to God's will. Thus, we have to force and condescend and change our will according to God's "who desires all men to be saved and to come to the knowledge of the truth." (1 Tim 2:4)

Let us think about it: we force ourselves to study in order to achieve our aim. We exert ourselves to exercise knowing that the result is beneficial. Same with the spiritual rule, we have to force ourselves to adhere to it with the knowledge that it is beneficial for us in our present lives and eternity.

It would be exasperating to feel enslaved to a compulsory rule, as if the rule is a cruel and merciless master! Why don't we feel that traffic light, for example, is burdensome? We adhere to its rules willingly without grumbling! For this reason it is essential to go over the aim of the Spiritual Canon in order to ensure that the aim is purely spiritual and not emotional. The clear intention of the aim facilitates to maintain it.

Therefore, the Spiritual Canon needs commitment besides spiritual leniency and freedom of will. We are convinced that we enforce the spiritual rule for its importance, with our free will, as it is essential for our salvation.

Not adhering to the Spiritual Canon is dangerous, as we would drift away from God because of our neglect. This is similar to a student who does not study, so the expected result is that he would fail in his exam.

We force ourselves to gain many things in our daily lives for our own good. We eat at a particular hour or take medicine, even if it is against our will. So why wouldn't we force ourselves to what is spiritual and important to our eternal salvation?

VI - SPIRITUAL CANON AND THE FEELING OF RESPONSIBILITY

Besides the freedom of abiding by the spiritual rule, it is inevitable that this freedom be accompanied by responsibility (success or failure) "you were faithful over a few things, I will make you ruler over many things. Enter into the joy of your Lord." (Matt 25:21) We are responsible to abide by these rules, not only for our own salvation but for others as well. As we have inherited them from our forefathers, hence it is our responsibility to pass them on to others, so that the blessed fathers' experiences may be passed on from one generation to the other.

As traffic lights regulate traffic and ensure our safety and the safety of others, so is the Spiritual Canon. This regulates our walk with God; without which we would have no guidelines to follow!

Thus, spiritual rules place responsibility on us; to keep and abide by them and pass them unto others to follow. It is not enough to consider our own salvation but it is our responsibility to ensure that others taste the beauty of abiding by a spiritual rule.

VII - GROWTH IN THE
SPIRITUAL CANON

As long as the Spiritual Canon is working with the spirit, it is inevitable that it matures gradually; this varies from one person to another. In spite of this maturity, there could come a period of fluctuation, depending on several circumstances.

Growth in the Spiritual Canon is not measured by 'how many' are our spiritual practises, but rather 'how' it is accomplished, in other words the methods by which these are practised. Growth is measured by the depth of understanding and by experience; as St Paul says, "When I was a child, I spoke as a child, I understood as a child, I thought as a child; but when I became a man, I put away childish things." (1 Cor 13:11)

Spiritual Canon is the spiritual food by which we are

spiritually nurtured. The more we practise it, the more we mature spiritually. It is said about our Lord Jesus Christ in His humanity, "And Jesus increased in wisdom and stature, and in favour with God and men" (Luke 2:52)

We are expected to be perfect, as our Lord is perfect. Thus, it is inevitable to constantly grow in our spiritual practice, as it is the ladder by which we climb gradually to a better spiritual level.

There is a Spiritual Canon for the beginners, another for the mediocre and a high levelled for the experienced, of whom St Paul refers to as, "those who by reason of use have their senses exercised to discern both good and evil." (Heb 5:14)

This maturity signifies that we are constantly growing and enjoying a special relationship with the Lord and feeling His presence in our lives.

Our Lord Jesus Christ gives us great hope by saying, "In My Father's house are many mansions;" (John 14:2) And St Paul also stresses on the same point, "for one star differs from another star in glory." (1 Cor 15:41) From these we learn that we have to try to reach the required standard, which will allow us to gain a place prepared for those who are committed in their spiritual struggle.

Our main aim in life is to be with the Lord. How can we make this possible? The answer is: by constantly lifting our hearts, minds and souls to our Lord; adhere to our spiritual rule with love and dedication and to ensure that we continually mature in our spiritual journey.

VIII - SPIRITUAL CANON AND SELF EXAMINATION

We should always examine ourselves according to the principles of the Spiritual Canon. When doing so, we have to look at the method of recitation, not only on the amount. More important than how many we prayed we should consider the spiritual level by which we recited our prayers.

It is advisable to stop from time to time and examine our conscious in order to find out whether we are committed to the Spiritual Canon or have we drifted. We might discover hidden sins like languor, self-righteousness, day dreaming, arrogance, self-indulgence that obstruct our walk with the Lord. As soon as we discover any sin we should repent, with tears and sorrow, for drifting away from our spiritual rule.

We have to realise that the Spiritual Canon is an antidote against Satan's intrigues and a weapon by which we fight him. It is also the medicine by which we are cured of all kinds of spiritual deceases. Therefore, it is dangerous if we are careless or apathetic in keeping the rule, which was set for our spiritual progress.

Moreover, not only are we to consider the rule of prayer, reading the Bible, fasting and genuflecting, but we should always examine ourselves on the rules of obedience, love, silence, purity, perseverance, humility, patience, self-control. We should also be mindful of the rules of compassion, affection and all actions and deeds.

In the monastery these are called "Rules of Obedience"

IX - WARS THAT OBSTRUCT THE SPIRITUAL CANON

Satan tries by all means to manoeuvre us to postpone or delay the Spiritual Canon. This proves how Satan fears our commitment in preserving the Spiritual Canon. Even if the rule is simple, still Satan abhors anything to do with loyalty to the Lord.

Wars from Satan:

1.   *Enslavement to the Spiritual Canon!*
Satan tries to convince us that our devotion to the rules enslaves us. And that we did not set these rules ourselves but they

were enforced on us by others. So why should we be committed in keeping them?

These intrigues are no doubt irrational, as no person can force another to adhere to a certain rule without his consent. The spiritual father in confession introduces these rules without compelling or forcing the person to abide by them. This is similar to like a doctor who prescribes medicine and it is up to the person to take it or not; all is left to the free will of the individual.

Hence, we practise the Spiritual Canon with acceptance and with our own free will "for we are not ignorant of his devices." (2 Cor 2:11) We should always be wary of the source of falling in Satan's trap. That is why we should always be awake and force ourselves to stick to our spiritual rules, under all circumstances.

Anyone who claims that he does not want to enslave himself to any rule, this person is actually enslaving himself to his own desires. A good example is the 'Prodigal Son', who felt that he was enslaved and tight up in his father's house. He asked for his freedom, away from his father's confinement, to live a liberated life, away from any commitment. What was the result of this freedom? He was enslaved to people, shepherding the pigs, yearning to eat from their food! At last he realised the false dreams set by the devil's intrigues! He humbly asked to go back to his father.

Let us ask ourselves: Why do we commit ourselves to adhere to all natural rules of the body and other factors, with contentment and joy, without feeling that we are enslaved to them, but when it comes to the Spiritual Canon we doubt and find difficulty to adhere to its rules and be committed? If Satan tries to put it in our minds that we are enslaved to Spiritual Canon! Let us fight him with the same words Jesus used: Away with you, Satan! For I shall worship the Lord my God, and Him only will I worship. (Matt 4:10)

Are there any loses or gains behind preserving the Spiritual Canon? Certainly there are gains and no losses, even when we keep them unwillingly as we do in daily matters, such as education, eating, and taking medicine?

Let us consider the following: Do we need to force ourselves to stand in front of God in prayers, or hear His voice in the Holy Bible? On the other hand, do we need forcing to stand in front of a manager at work or any important person? Who deserves more esteem, God or humans?

Do we really deserve to stand in front of God and talk to Him? Who deserves to enter the House of God and receive His body and blood? Why don't we feel that the Spiritual Canon is a great blessing and preserve it with great joy? This is Satan's deceitful and false war. He is aware of the power of Spiritual Canon. He knows that it is the weapon and medicine in the hands of any believer; so he tries by any means to obstruct these rules.

Let us not allow Satan to deceive us! There is a great difference between 'forcing' and 'enslaving'. Forcing is done by our own will power; but slavery is forced on us. The difficulty is that we have not reached the stage where we have surrendered our will completely to the will of God; where we can say with the Lord, "not My will, but Yours, be done"

Most of the saints forced themselves, at the beginning, to abide by Spiritual Canon; until it became part of their lives.

No longer could they live without it, as they favoured it above everything else.

It is said that the secret of Pope Kyrolous VI sainthood is that, throughout his life, he meticulously abided by the rules he set for himself: praying the Agbia, the Bible, praises, Vespers and the holy Liturgy.

It is also known of the late Anba Daniel, Bishop of Khartoum, that he never neglected the Spiritual Canon not even for one day in his entire life!

Same with the late Anba Maximus Bishop of Kalobia, whenever he visited any monastery, he would excuse himself and enter any cell and pray in the designated time, then come out.

What scares Satan the most is our commitment to our Spiritual Canon. He knows that it is our protection, weapon and comfort. The saints proclaim that keeping the Spiritual Canon, even if we are not aware of its power, Satan is still terrified by it.

Our forefathers said, 'if we pray only when we desire to pray, we will never pray.' We have to force ourselves at the beginning, until we get used to it.

Commitment to the Spiritual Canon is similar to a soldier who persists in his daily exercises, even during the time of peace, so that he may be prepared in the time of war.

2.   *Apathy and Boredom*

Many of us encounter this war - if not all of us! We feel bored and apathetic and lack the desire to continue. We try to rush our prayers in order to finish quickly. The saints try to encourage and advice, to continue praying, even when bored, as it is better than nothing. This will be an acceptable sacrifice in front of the Lord. "Present your bodies a living sacrifice, holy, acceptable to God, which is your reasonable service." (Rom 12:1)

This sort of period could implant humility and perseverance in our hearts. The most important thing is that we have to go back, even gradually to the Spiritual Canon.

It is advisable during such time to come closer to the father in confession so that he may encourage and assist us. The priest may even change a bit of the Spiritual Canon or even swap it with a different rule.

3.   Pride

We find this in the example of the Pharisee and the Tax-Collector. (Luke 18:9-14) The Pharisee kept some spiritual rules in prayer, fasting and giving tithes. He was self-righteous and looked down on others. But he was not righteous in the sight of God. Consider what is written in Luke 17:10, "When you have done all those things which you are commanded, say, 'We are unprofitable servants. We have done what was our duty to do.' What have we to be proud of? Are we doing God a favour by keeping our prayer rules? Not at all! This is the least duty we can do! We are still lacking when we compare ourselves to others, who are more righteous than we are.

4.   Waste of time

Satan has a way of occupying our time in various things so that we cannot find time to keep our Spiritual Canon. We can call this 'postponing war'. This 'postponing' never comes to an end! It always comes with the slogan 'yes, I'll do it later.' And this 'later' never comes!

How we wish we could learn never to postpone our Spiritual Canon; and keep it as our first priority! After which we can do whatever we wish! It is written," What profit is it to a man if he gains the whole world, and loses his own soul?" (Matt 16:26)

What else can be more important than meeting our Lord and speaking to Him in prayers? How much precious time do we waste without gaining anything? Or else spend our time the wrong way, which is harmful to us or to others!! Sometimes this is a means of escape from keeping the Spiritual Canon or laziness or doing earthly things, which interest us more! We then find no time for our spiritual work! What a pity!

If we claim that we have no time, let us go over our daily schedule and find out how much time have we wasted in trivial matters! How much time have we spent on the phone chatting to friends, or in front of the television or the computer? We find' time for every other thing but when it comes to the word of God we create excuses of not having enough time! Are we greater than David who said, "Seven times a day I praise You,"(Ps119:163) or "I will not give sleep to my eyes Or slumber to my eyelids, Until I find a place for the Lord,' (Ps132:4-5) also in Psalm 27:4 he says, "One thing I have desired of the Lord, That will I seek: That I may dwell in the house of the Lord All the days of my life, To behold the beauty of the Lord, And to inquire in His temple."

We have to understand that postponing, neglecting or wasting time are all wars from Satan, who hates to see us talk to God. We have to understand that time is short, and the hour that passes can never be retrieved! Why do we neglect the enjoyment of a close relationship with the Lord, and waste time on perishable matters?

Serving in church should never be an excuse for not performing our Spiritual Canon. We can serve as much as we like, be it Sunday School or any other church service, but these should never delay our duty to spend precious time underneath the feet of the Lord, like Mary, and pour fragrant oil on His blessed head, proclaiming our love and desire to be close to Him! We have to be cautious not to be like a husband who spends all his time at work and never finds time to talk to his wife or children!

5.   *Day Dreaming*

This is the worst war against mankind! Our brains do not stop thinking! As soon as a spiritual thought comes, our minds roam to other earthy affairs! These come as a result of our scattered thoughts on various sensual matters or maybe worries or tribulations.

For these reasons, we ought to practice our Spiritual Canon at a suitable time in a quiet place, when our thoughts are calm. We have to try hard to control our thoughts and stay focused and pray from the depth of our hearts.

Even if we pray while day-dreaming, it is better than not praying at all! Keeping our spiritual rule will help gather our thoughts. The holy fathers' advice that reading would help solve the problem of scattered thoughts. Reading will assist us to concentrate more than praying.

We need to be meticulous in keeping our thoughts clear from worldly matters - and try to prepare ourselves spiritually, before preceding with our Spiritual Canon.

6.   *Pretentious & Self-Righteousness*

It is written in the Holy Bible, "Everyone who is among you, not to think of himself more highly than he ought to think, but to think soberly," (Ro 12:3)

The holy Fathers say "middle way has saved many"

Showing off in excess prayers, fasting, asceticism, prostrations, and all kinds of spiritual exercises, cause greater harm than good, physically and spiritually! These could cause satanic visions and great disturbances. The devil rejoices and prompts us not to reveal these highly spiritual acts to the father in confession or else the confession father will be jealous of our highly spiritual status, which he lacks!

This happened to one of the monks, when the devil appeared to him in the form of an angel and praised his great spirituality, asceticism and holiness. He promised that he would come the following day, with other angels, and meet him on the roof of the monastery, where they will carry him on a fiery chariot, like Elijah. Satan advised him not to reveal this secret to anyone, especially to his father in confession. The poor conceited monk believed the devil!

The following day he waited on the roof and as soon as he saw the fiery chariot, he rejoiced with pride, and as soon as he put his feet in, he dropped five meters to the ground. Because of God's mercy he had time to repent and confess before he gave up his spirit.

There is a great difference between the extreme pretentiousness, which proceeds from pride, and the visit of grace, which is from God. Thus, the holy fathers teach us that obedience to our father in confession surpasses prayers with arrogance and self-righteousness.

We have to bear in mind that 'obedience' and 'humility' are the fruits of the Spiritual Canon. How many people exerted themselves but were misled because of their arrogance and self-righteousness? Why? Because their effort was not built on humility and obedience! These are the two qualities that are outstanding in the Spiritual Canon.

Therefore, spiritual growth should be gradual and orderly and under the guidance of those who are more spiritually experienced.

7.   Sense of Exhaustion and Fatigue

Fatigue is one of the obstacles that obstructs our spiritual walk. Sometimes we postpone our Spiritual Canon to the end of the day; we then find that exhaustion and fatigue deprive us of continuing our spiritual duty. Sometimes this tiredness is a result of illness, so we ought to be cautious. But often it is bodily exhaustion, war from Satan, to delay our promptness to the Spiritual Canon. The feeling of tiredness comes especially while we are praying, reading the Bible or attending Mass. When Satan succeeds in his trick we find ourselves afterwards lively and wide awake, and could even spend the rest of the night watching television or in front of the computer!

A certain monk, whenever he used to stand up for prayers would feel feverish and shivering. When he would persist in his prayers both the fever and shiver would disappear. Obviously it was war from Satan!

8.   Diversion from the Main Target

Satan tries to make the Spiritual Canon an aim in itself. We feel disheartened if we are unable to continue practising it, or become proud if we persist in keeping it. Worst still is when we become hypocrites, like the Pharisees, and look for people's praise and admiration.

Sometimes we can become weary and question the benefits and advantages of the Spiritual Canon! We try to convince ourselves that we have prayed a lot, read the Bible from cover to cover, attended endless liturgies, listened to hundreds of sermons but still cannot feel any benefits or improvement in our spirituality! We question ourselves: Why force ourselves to do things that we do not benefit from? We then become discouraged and feel that we are not advancing spiritually but rather deteriorating.

Worst still is when Satan tempts us to compare ourselves to people of the world. He lures us to believe that those people live with no restrictions or rules, have no principles to guide them, but they live freely and enjoy life to the fullest. They seem very happy and successful with no worries at all! So why should we be restricted with laws and principles and deprive ourselves of the happiness these people are enjoying?

We have to bear in mind, that the devil will try his best to make us doubt. He will try to make us suspicious in the credibility of the Spiritual Canon. He will entice us by ideas such as: what prove do we have of its reliability? Be ready to backstab Satan! Can we prove that unperceivable things exist? We cannot see the result with our eyes but we can perceive its result. For example can we deny the benefits gained from eating? When we eat can we perceive the food nourishing the body, which help us grow? Again can we see the sickness being removed from the body, when medicine is applied? No, we cannot; but we can perceive the benefit of the medicine. Same with the Spiritual Canon its benefits are seen in the long run.

For these reasons we ought to be very careful to abide by our spiritual rules and never leave room for doubt or divert from our main target, which is everlasting life with the Lord. We have to fight the devil's intrigues!

9. *Keeping the Spiritual Canon a Secret*
Under the pretext of keeping our Spiritual Canon a secret, we neglect praying! Thus we reach the stage where instead of hiding the Spiritual Canon we cancel it altogether!

The only reason for keeping our Spiritual Canon a secret is that we may not gain praise or esteem from others. But it is dangerous if hiding it would hinder our prayers! It is pointless to hide the rule when everyone around is following the same canon; example in a monastery where every monk reads Agbaia, Praises, obedience, etc all monks are prompt in abiding by them. In this case there is no need for secrecy!

Our Lord taught us to do all deeds in secret. If this is taken as an excuse, so that we do not perform our spiritual duty, that would be a trick from Satan to delay our spiritual rule.

10. *Physical Torture*
This kind of war attacks those who are well advanced in spirituality. Satan tortures the person physically, as in the case of Saint Anthony or with certain illness, as in the case of Job.

These wars show how much Satan is outraged with the Spiritual Canon. The saints say, "Even if you are not aware of the strength of prayer, the devil knows its power and fears it."

The fathers also say, "When Satan finds the thought and heart preoccupied with God's word and cannot find his way in, he attacks the body" This kind of war attacks only the very advanced in spirituality. How many of the holy fathers have we read about, who used to be tortured physically during prayer time?

X - SPIRITUAL CANON ACCORDING TO ST ISAAC THE SYRIAN

St Isaac the Syrian teaches: "Each level, in the spiritual life, depends wholly on the previous, from which it extends its strength and stability. Thus each time a person reaches a certain level he moves to a higher one preserving the previous ones he gained. If a person loses one of these degrees, no way will he reach the next level."

Again St Isaac said: "Don't you know that each spiritual exercise has its value? Every work has its direction? Every step has its specific time? Each circumstance has its own occasion? If anyone tries to reach what is beyond his capability, at the wrong time, he will not gain anything but on the contrary, he might harm himself."

From the above we learn that it is essential to take the advice of the experienced, to ensure that we are following the right spiritual path, acceptable to the Lord.

The Spiritual Canon, however small, if completed with persistence, at its designated time, and prayed at a suitable pace, without rushing, would have great power which automatically elevates the person. One might reach a higher spiritual level without feeling, as it is a gradual process.

To attain physical stamina, this needs time and continuous exercise. What about training ourselves to attain virtues? This too needs constant training in order to please God's heart.

Saint Isaac also said: "The spirit is naturally more precious than the body. Thus its work is greater than the body." He stresses that we need to understand, appreciate and elevate our spirituality above what is materialistic, as the latter is perishable but the spirit is eternal. To do so we need to be guided by a person who has experienced and reached such a level of spirituality, who would help us in our walk and guide us to persevere in the Spiritual Canon.

Saint Isaac compares this to a chain of practices and exercises, attached one to the other, if one part is undone the whole lot will scatter!

Saint Isaac, therefore, advises, "Have pity on yourself, my brother, and don't be too harsh on yourself, otherwise, you will hinder the good you have attained and become like a spiritual chain attached one to the other. Pay heed lest your excess ambition leads you to exhaustion, which will hinder your walk. Eat moderately or else you will crave to eat all the time. Do not step more than you are capable, or else you will not be able to continue walking,"

Saint Isaac warns against the war of self-righteousness, where a person overloads himself with spiritual practices, beyond his spiritual ability. He advises that small, persistent portion of prayer is better than immense segments which eventually discontinue.

Furthermore, St Isaac warns that not all rules are suitable for all. Some are suitable for the spiritually advanced and others for beginners. A canon suitable for a saint would not be suitable for an ordinary spiritual person. That is why it is important to consult the father in confession before commencing on any big spiritual task.

There are certain tasks that God gives to particular people, such as missionary work or evangelism, which are not suitable for everyone. For example monasticism is different to missionary work or evangelising in the world. What was appropriate for Saint Paul, for example, would not be suitable for an anchorite.

Thus St Isaac stresses that it is essential that we should attain the virtue of 'discernment' or 'spiritual enlightenment' so that we might be able to distinguish precisely between these matters.

There are common virtues such as love, patience, tolerance, humility etc, they are all perfect and need to be practiced by all. On the other hand, there are other virtues some of which are: silence, vigil, missionary work etc. these should be carried by special people and practiced at specific times.

In addition, St Isaac does not limit his advice on practising what is externally obvious only, but also focuses on the inner thoughts behind some actions. For example he does not stop at "Do not rebuke those who offend you" But continues, "But rather put the blame on yourself and reprimand yourself." He further advises, "Stay away from gossip and useless talk, as this extinguishes the spiritual movement which God implanted in your heart."

Saint Isaac wants to stress that virtues are essential, but at the same time the external circumstances and daily behaviour should be in accordance with the person's spiritual role. A monk, who lives a communal life, is different to the anchorite, who lives in the wilderness. A Christian who lives in the world is different to the evangelist or preacher. Each one of these has specific order and special role. Each has what is suitable and what will help him grow spiritually. All these come under the trait of 'Christian Virtues', which is essential for our salvation.

Furthermore, St Isaac advices on the importance of praying the psalms, fasting, and reading the Holy Bible. He adds that the method of implementation changes from one person to another, according to the person's spiritual need and status. All these lead us once more to the importance of the spirit of discernment and the guidance of the spiritual fathers, who experienced this route before us.

What was said in this booklet is a general idea of the

Spiritual Canon and the various points of views associated with it. There are many other experiences concerning this topic, but it is left to the person to decide, according to his spiritual level.

The spiritual life cannot be studied but rather lived! It is a personal experience of life. Our Spiritual Canon could be similar to others, but it will be practised differently from one person to another, according to his spiritual status.

There has to be a clear aim in order to advance forward. Spiritual Canon is not a rule to be kept but to be lived. It is not static but rather active, movable, lively and a lenient rule. "God is Spirit, and those who worship Him must worship in spirit and truth." (John 4:24)

The angels in heaven worship God. They serve Him with proficiency and efficiency. In spite of that, they do their job with freedom, joy and interest. Their eternal happiness is complete by performing such jobs, which is the foundation of their incessant love for God.

Thus the Spiritual Canon is an expression of love. God Himself expresses His love for us efficiently and not haphazardly! "For God is not the author of confusion but of peace, as in all the churches of the saints." (1 Cor 14:33)

May God bless us with His continuous presence through the Spiritual Canon and lead our lives to constant joy, to live with Him in eternal bliss. Amen

www.ingramcontent.com/pod-product-compliance
Lightning Source LLC
Chambersburg PA
CBHW021916040426
42447CB00007B/884